Juggling for the Complete Klutz

Juggling for the Complete Klutz

By John Cassidy and B.C. Rimbeaux
Illustrated By Diane Waller

Juggling for the Complete Klutz
and the "book and bag"
packaging format, are U.S.
registered trademarks.

ISBN 0-932592-00-7

Third edition

Printed in the United States of America

Published by
• Klutz Press •
Palo Alto, California

Dedicated to the closet klutzes of the world.

FOREWORD

J*UGGLING FOR THE C*OMPLETE K*LUTZ*, which celebrates the sale of its millionth copy in this new edition, started life in 1977 as a humble lesson plan for a sophomore English class at Mountain View High School, Mountain View, California.

That was in 1977. I was a student teacher losing in my daily battle for 24 wandering attention spans. Juggling was something I had learned at college and then refined a bit during summers where I led river rafting trips. All the guides were expected to be at least marginally entertaining around the campfire. Juggling was my humble contribution.

That first mimeographed copy was handed out one Friday period when any chance for real education had long since evaporated in the afternoon, post-lunch brain-haze. I passed out 75 used tennis balls to supplement the lesson and the resulting chaos reminded me of an animated science cartoon I once saw of random molecular motion.

From that point on, juggling lessons became the Friday afternoon staple. I fleshed out the mimeo lesson plan and started substituting bean bags for tennis balls in an effort to reduce the chaos factor. It wasn't long before I had a classful of aspiring circus stars.

Shortly after that, a couple of friends and I ran off three thousand copies of JUGGLING and distributed them via the bicycle and backpack system. When they sold, the three of us, Darrell Hack, B.C. Rimbeaux, and I sat down to count our profits (some $35), assess our future and dream the American entrepreneurial dream —juggling version.

Thus was formed Klutz Press.

The edition you're holding here is the 35th printing and the second revision of JUGGLING FOR THE COMPLETE KLUTZ. The text has been updated in a few spots, corrections that should have been made years ago have finally been made, and most importantly, the section on juggling with clubs has been expanded quite a bit to reflect its growing popularity.

As an activity, juggling has started to infiltrate the mainstream of American foolishness. It's now quite common to find otherwise normal people who can casually pick up three apples, go through a little 3-object razzmatazz, then wrap it all up with an apple sauce finale. We like to think we've played some small role in this cultural development.

The first edition of *JUGGLING* set forth our goals in a short preface. We stand by them still.

"For centuries juggling has been a performers' art. The little trick of getting the three objects to dance around your hands has always managed to keep a small sense of magic about it.

Our purpose in writing this book however, is to take juggling off the stage and pass it around.

It is our belief that juggling really isn't a spectator sport. It's one form of insanity we feel everyone has a right to experience." *

So you're interested in learning how to juggle but it took you four years to learn how to tie your shoes, and besides, dropping things has always been second nature to you. When your class played softball, you were always last picked and then packed off to right field. Your mother always puts away breakables whenever you step into the house. You're an original klutz and you probably think juggling is only for the super-coordinated.

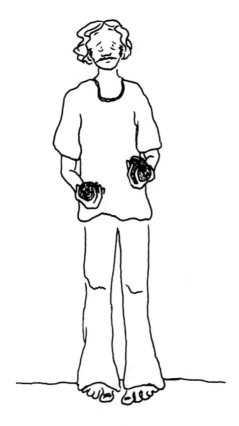

RELAX. Most people have got the moves down and are well on their way to juggling after only fifteen minutes, and even hard-core cases like you won't be far behind.

It's **SIMPLE!** The motions are new and for the first couple of minutes they feel as awkward as brushing your teeth left-handed, but the truth is — they're easy, and anyone can do it.

As for the question of Why? I can only mumble vaguely about the unknowable nooks and crannies of the human spirit. Or relate to you those times when I've found juggling to be just the answer for that slack moment or awkward minute. Perhaps you sometimes find yourself at a loss for a good "leave-'em-really-impressed" kind of parting line? At a job interview perhaps, or on a first date, what could be more appropriate? My own experience suggests that hitch-hiking may be the one arena where the juggler has a distinct advantage over his non-juggling competitor. Who could resist a little side-of-the-road razzle-dazzle?

Although the motions aren't difficult, they should be absorbed in bite-sized little chunks. Otherwise you'll run afoul of frustration, something that I will talk about a little later. In the meantime, read through the first three steps and glance at the pictures before picking up the bags. Don't bother reading about the problems just yet. They won't make sense until you have them anyway.

STEP I: The Drop

Pick up all three bags and hold them, briefly. You'll note that there is one more bag than you have hands, unless you are that rather rare case, in which event send away for our limited edition of *Juggling for the Exceptionally Gifted*.

Throw all three bags into the air and making no effort to catch any of them, let them all hit the ground. This is an example of **THE DROP.** I do it all the time and so will you, but it's good to familiarize yourself with the moves early on. Practice **THE DROP** until the novelty wears off. Many people find this occurs quite rapidly, others seem to get a lot out of this exercise for quite some time. Leaving those folks to themselves, we'll move on.

STEP II: The Toss

Put two bags away for a time and hold just one. Cradle it in the center of your hand, *not on your fingers.* (Read that last line again. It's more important than you think.)

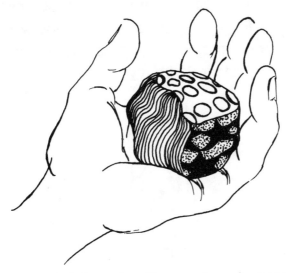

You should be standing, relaxed, even grinning perhaps, your elbows near your body and your hands at about waist height. Toss the bag in easy arcs about as high as your eyes and as wide as your body, back and forth, hand to hand. It won't take you long to discover that this exercise is only a hair more interesting than the first, but you should keep at it a little longer. The important thing is to keep your tosses consistent, one after the other, so that you don't have to go lunging around catching weird throws.

Don't make your throws stiffly either. Use a kind of "scooping" motion, as in the illustration. Ideally, you should be able to "scoop" a toss up and have it land — eyes closed — in your other hand. Realistically, if you can make the catch without having to dive for it, you'll be doing about normally.

Do this one until it gets boring. A minute seems to be about the limit for most people, but push yourself for a little more. Ignore those snickers from your audience, it's only the rawest kind of envy.

Figure 1: The "Scoop" Toss

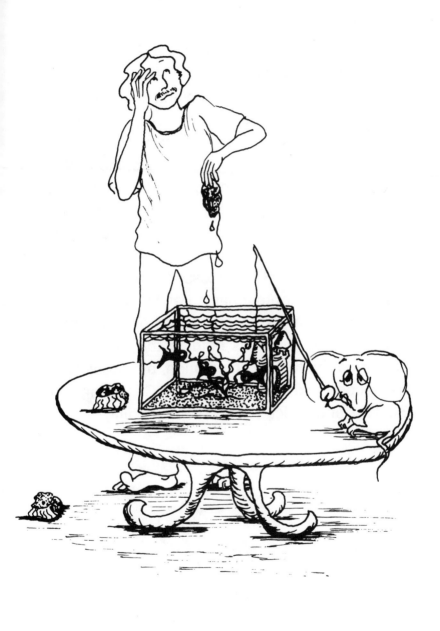

STEP III: The Exchange

This is THE step, so pay attention. Read it all the way through before you do anything rash.

Pick up a second bag and cradle it in your hand so that you now have a bag in each hand. Look at *figure 2* for an idea of what's going to happen here. I'll try to explain at the same time by hitting some of the key points and then going over some of the common problems — but don't let all the coaching throw you. Remember, it's a new motion so it's awkward at first, but persevere.

Using your best STEP II toss, throw one bag up and over toward your other hand. Let it come to the top of its arc, and then, just as it starts to drop down into your other hand — which is holding the second bag — exchange the two, in one motion, by "scoop-tossing" the second and catching the first. Confusing, isn't it? But look at the pictures and keep reading.

The First Toss
Your hand should
move in a little
scooping motion.

a.

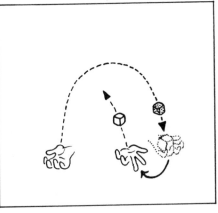

The Exchange
Your hand swings
in to make the
toss and out to
make the catch.

b.

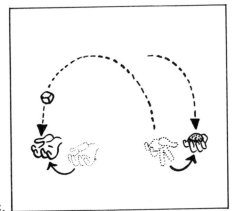

The Grand Finale

Figure 2

c.

17

Your second toss should pass to the inside of the first so that both throws ARE IN THE SAME PLANE RIGHT THERE IN FRONT OF YOU. Also, the path of the second toss should look the same as the first in terms of height and width. And remember, that second toss should not happen until the first has passed through the top of its arc. Otherwise, you will create all kinds of havoc. The exchange should be one smooth toss-and-catch motion.

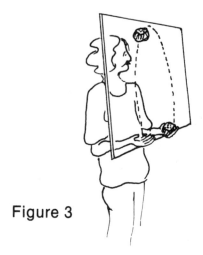

Figure 3

All right. That's the way it's supposed to happen. But go ahead and work at it for a little bit and then come back and I'll talk about how it *really* happened when you tried it. Incidentally, your first ten or so attempts are going to look and feel just terrible, so you might as well get used to that one right away. But take heart, a mere ten minutes or so generally makes a big difference.

You're back, right? And you've got some problems. I know the feeling well, but read on. Help is on the way.

THE PANIC RESPONSE

The most popular problem. You'll throw the second bag into the bleachers. Impossible to catch. Or, if you're under a little better control, you'll have to stretch to full arm's length to make the second grab.

This is an obnoxious problem that you probably have. The solution is ironclad mental control. This is what is happening in your nervous system as you go through this routine.

Your first throw goes up in a nice arc. Suddenly, your brain realizes that the hand that is going to have to make the catch...*is already occupied! Panic!!* A neural alarm flashes down to your occupied hand: "Collision emergency! Get rid of that other bag! Throw it anywhere, but *CLEAR THAT LANDING SPACE!*"

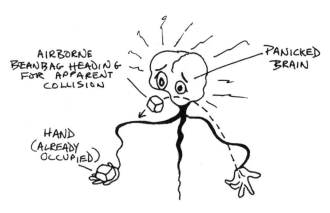

This is totally unnecessary. There's plenty of time to make a nice controlled scoop-toss, but your brain over-reacts. Get a grip on yourself. Concentrate on your second toss. Swing your hand in, throw the bag up in a nice controlled arc just to the inside of the dropping bag, and then swing your hand back out to make the catch. You know you've done it perfectly when the second toss lands in your hand. No reaching. It all happens in a single plane (in other words, you should be able to do it right in front of a wall without banging your knuckles).

Some people respond differently to this problem of one bag heading for an already occupied hand. They have more control than that. Instead of panicking, they have

THE CHEAT RESPONSE

For these people, when they see the first toss heading in for a landing on top of the other bag, it's no problem, they cheat. They clear the landing area by

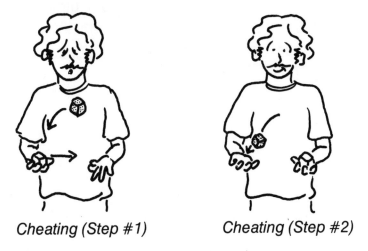

Cheating (Step #1)   *Cheating (Step #2)*

just handing that bag over. Back to the first hand. Then they think they've done something clever.

THE SECOND TOSS GOES UP! NOT ACROSS! Look at the illustrations.

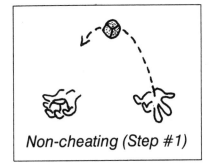

Non-cheating (Step #1)

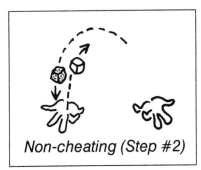

Non-cheating (Step #2)

21

OK. Enough words. Try your exchanges for 15 drops. Then take a break and try again for another 15. When you're starting to get the hang of it going one way (in other words, your first toss always comes out of one particular hand) switch. Start with your other hand. Give that one 15 drops and take another break. If everything still feels just terrible, take a look at Step V: Special Problems.

STEP IV: The Jug

The hardest thing about STEP IV is knowing when to go for it. If you've got your exchanges down — in both hands — then this is just the wrap-up. So ask yourself if you're feeling pretty smooth before you jump into this one.

You are? Fine, you're home free. You may not have realized it, but you already know the basic juggling moves. So take a deep breath and pick up all three bags. Imagine for a moment how this amazing thing is going to look. Starting with your two-bag hand, you're going to give one of the bags a good toss and suddenly it'll be in the air, arching over toward your other hand. Meanwhile, you're still going to be holding one bag in each hand. Now as this flying bag begins to drop down into your hand, you should recognize a familiar scene. Exchange the flier with the held bag which then goes to the top of *its* arc, and as *it* starts to come in for a landing, you exchange *it* for the other held bag which then begins its little trip.

As you're doing this, it'll probably help to count out loud to yourself. Throwing the first bag up is "1", the second bag is "2", the third bag "3", and for the moment at least, that should be plenty.

Note: Just because I didn't put all the dotted hands in this illustration doesn't mean you should stop doing the "scoop-toss" thing. I just figured you'd gotten the point by now and besides, I didn't want to mess up the drawing.

a.

b.

The First Toss

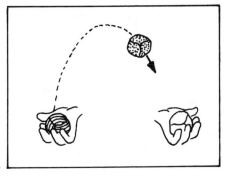

c.

The First Exchange

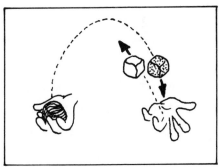

d.

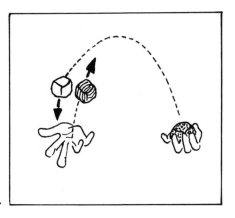

The Second Exchange
Note that your hands weave back and forth ("scoop tossing") so that the up-going bag can avoid the down-going one.

If you can do this much, take a low bow. You're JUGGLING!!! All this time you thought juggling was keeping two or three things in the air at once. Now you should be able to see that there's really one *one* thing flying around — the others are just being held until they get exchanged with the flier, one at a time.

If you can put two exchanges back to back, I call that a "jug." Two jugs would be four exchanges in a row without a drop.

Once you can do a jug there'll be no stopping you. But let me explain what will undoubtedly start happening. In the heat of the moment you'll forget to concentrate on your tosses and they'll begin to fly out away from you, resulting in the "sprinting juggler syndrome."

When this starts to happen (and don't worry, it happens to everyone) remember what you learned about keeping your exchanges in one plane by tossing each bag to the *inside* of the dropping bag's arc. And don't start using your whole arm to make your tosses either. Keep your elbows pretty close to your sides and your hands at about waist height. Practice in front of a wall if you want, but......CONCENTRATE ON WHERE YOU'RE PUTTING THOSE TOSSES!

To continue on in this vein is to run the risk of becoming a nag. And so I will leave you with no more warning than this: take frequent breaks while you're trying to learn. Twenty minutes spent in two ten minute spurts is much more effective than in one lump.

And when all else fails, remember these few words whose wisdom has guided me through more than just a few trying times: "It's always darkest just before it gets pitch black."

STEP V: Special Problems

Most everyone seems to have a strong tendency to turn to this section too soon. Deep in our hearts we all figure we're exceptional — one way or another — and consequently deserving of some special attention.

It is often a deeply humbling experience to realize that our problems are neither very unusual, nor even very serious. So I will try to break this to you as gently as I can. If you've been trying for ten minutes or so and are still dropping a lot or having trouble keeping all the action right there in front of you (here it comes, so steel yourself), you're probably doing quite well — just suffering from a mild shortage of practice. Try it for a little longer and then take a break. You'll get less frustrated that way and it will give your muscles a chance to think about it all.

After a little while, pick up the bags and try it again with renewed concentration. If it still doesn't click at all, read on and see if you can recognize whatever it is that's holding you up.

PROBLEM: You're on STEP III: THE EXCHANGE, with just two bags, but you can't seem to make it work. You flub up the toss, you flub up the catch...everything feels terrible, and you've tried and tried.

BEST SOLUTION: Go get yourself a friend — you probably need one about now anyhow — and have him stand next to you, shoulder to shoulder. You can hold hands if you want, or if you're not that kind of friends, you can put your inside hands behind your own backs.

With your outside hands you're going to be doing exchanges. This is how it goes:

Put a bag in your outside hand and one in your friend's. Toss your bag in a nice easy arc over to your friend. Just before it lands in his hand (it's occupied, right?), he should toss you his bag and catch yours — all in that one hand, don't forget. His throw should go underneath yours. Doing exchanges like this (with two people) should slow things down enough so that you can eliminate the element of panic from your tosses. Change places with your friend after a little while so that you can loosen up both hands.

If you and your friend happen to be a particularly smooth team, you might want to extend this exercise into something that might be called "Siamese-twin" juggling. All you have to do is add a third bag to the act, which quickens things up a bit, but not too badly. Instead of doing one exchange and stopping, you're going to be doing a bunch of exchanges back-to-back (or side-to-side as the case happens to be).

If you can get some kind of blasé expression on your faces while you're doing this, then you've got your first trick — which isn't bad progress at all.

SECOND BEST SOLUTION

Since this is really just a psychological problem, there are a couple of possible psychological solutions.

One that I have used with some success is the idea of throwing the second bag through an imaginary wire loop "attached" to the dropping bag.

Try this for one or two exchanges. At the finish of each exchange, stop and ask yourself if your throw went through the "loop". If it didn't, ask yourself by how much you missed. If you can tell yourself how far off you were, then you've got your concentration focussed on the right place, i.e. the placement of that second toss.

Another use of the same idea is to paint little targets on the palms of your hands. This can make for awkward explanations during the non-juggling portion of your day though, and I offer it only as a suggestion.

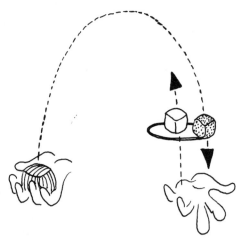

PROBLEM: You're on STEP IV: The Jug, and you are a serious sprinting juggler. There is no way you can keep your throws under control.

SOLUTION: First of all, practice in front of a wall so that you *can't* throw them too far out in front of you. An alternative to this: try it sitting down. (I've never found this to be so great, but everyone else says it helps, so I'll pass it on.) As a last resort you might try practicing on the edge of a cliff. A close friend of mine (rest his soul) used to swear by this one.

PROBLEM: Your legs are killing you from picking up your drops all the time.

SOLUTION: Stand over a table, hire a bag boy, *OR* BUILD YOUR OWN RETRIEVAL SKIRT (see picture for construction details).

Once you've smoothed out your three-bag juggling and can do it without having to dash across the room, you'll probably start wondering about the next step. Your friends, too, will be getting bored with your new little act. "What about four?" they'll ask innocently. Or even better, "How many can you do?" as if anything less than eleven would put them to sleep.

Juggling is not a spectator sport! If you want to be rid of these ingrates who don't know real talent when they see it, your only recourse is to stop juggling, hand them a bag and show them how to do THE TOSS. They'll be hooked in no time.

And once they are, you've got your partner for team juggling, which probably ought to be your first trick on your way to Ringling Brothers.

STEALING

You and your partner both ought to be at least fairly decent jugglers before you try this one. By that I mean you should each be able to do twenty or more jugs without dropping.

The ingredients for this trick are: two people and three juggling bags.

Let your partner begin this one. As he juggles merrily away, stand right beside him shoulder to shoulder, at the ready. For the first few attempts, this by itself will make him nervous enough to drop everything in hysterics. Once you've matured your way over that little hurdle, you can go on.

What you are going to do here is interrupt his juggling by taking two **successive** throws—one right after the other—just as they reach the tops of their arcs. That should leave you holding two bags. If your partner is cooperating, he can direct that third bag over your way. As it starts to drop into one of your (occupied) hands, just do an exchange—and you're off on your own, juggling away.

Be sure to start by taking a toss that comes out of your friend's outside hand with *your* outside hand. Then, on the very next toss, with your inside hand take the next bag (at the top of its arc), which should have come out of your friend's inside hand. As you're picking these bags off at the tops of their arcs, try to keep your palms up—you're catching these bags, not clawing them out of the air.

I realize this all sounds very complicated, but look at the diagrams and give it a try anyhow. Some things are a lot easier done than said.

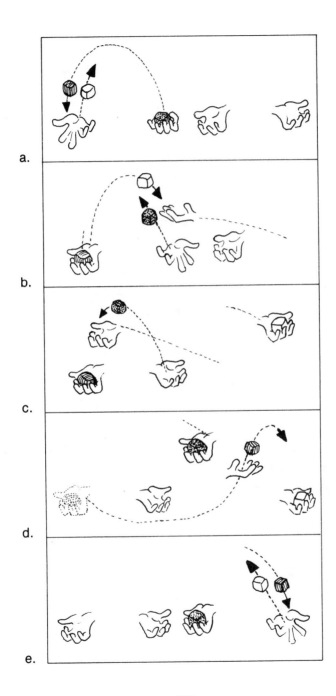

a.

b.

c.

d.

e.

PASSING

This is the basic part of team juggling and it requires two pretty smooth jugglers. In other words, each of you ought to be able to do thirty or more jugs without a drop and still maintain a relatively calm expression on your faces.

Ingredients: two of the aforementioned type jugglers, and six bean bags.

Arrange yourselves so that you're facing each other, a few feet apart. In your right hands put two bags, in your lefts, one. Each of you start juggling, but make an effort to start together and stay in time—in other words, synchronously. It helps a lot if one of you counts out loud every time a toss leaves your right hand, "1...2...3".

OK. On a pre-arranged number, say three, instead of tossing across to your *own* left hand, throw your bag in a nice, easy arc, over to your friend's *left* hand. And at the same time, he should be doing exactly the same thing.

If it works out, (and it won't for a while), both of you will juggle along, switch two bags, and continue juggling—all without really missing a beat.

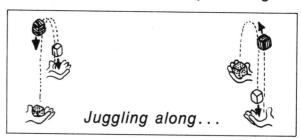

a.   *Juggling along...*

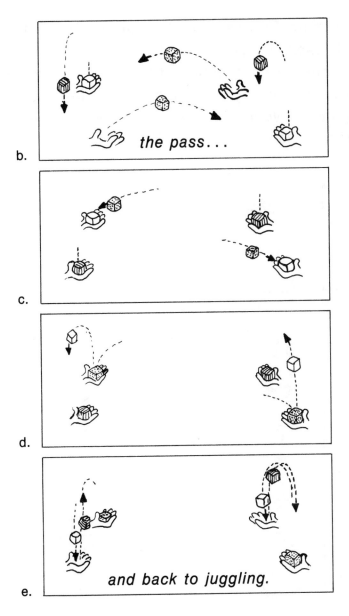

b.

the pass...

c.

d.

e.

and back to juggling.

It sounds tricky because it is, but there are a few warm-up exercises that can help.

Warm-up Exercise No. 1 While you're holding a bag in each hand, have your friend toss you a third — into your left hand. Before it lands, do an exchange and begin your own juggling. After a few moments juggling on your own, throw him one back — from your right hand — and stop.

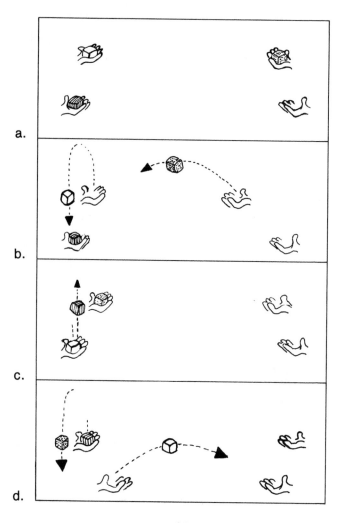

a.

b.

c.

d.

Warm-up Exercise No. 2 Start by holding three bags and giving your friend a fourth. Begin juggling (and counting) and then, on "three", make the toss over to your friend who — at the same time — should feed your hand with a nice easy toss. Your friend won't be juggling during this exercise. His job is strictly to catch your one toss while feeding you another. If it's done smoothly, you can juggle along without missing a beat.

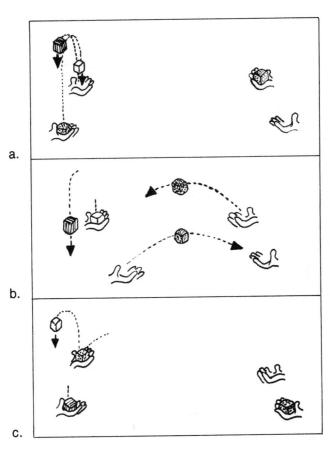

a.

b.

c.

Switch back and forth on all these exercises so that both of you can get it at the same time.

When you're by yourself, you can practice passing by standing in front of a wall and bouncing every third toss out of your right hand off the wall and into your left.

Just so you don't feel unusually handicapped, I'll describe the major problem that seems to get everyone when they try passing for the first time.

You'll be juggling along, both of you in time. On the third throw out of your right hand, you'll do it just the way you're supposed to. Both your right hand tosses will go across, you'll catch them, and then...chaos. The whole thing will fall apart because you'll try to throw the next one over there too. Meanwhile, your partner's going through the same thing. Mass confusion.

It's another psychological problem. You're in the habit of keeping all your tosses to yourself. You break it for one toss over to your partner, and then...you can't get back into the old rut, and you panic.

As usual, the cure is practice. If you're not too proud to go backwards, exercise No. 2, described above, is the least painful way to get it.

There will come a time, perhaps even in your lifetime, when you'll be able to execute this passing

trick with a certain amount of flair. Repeatedly,
even.

This then, is the time for graduation ceremonies. Instead of just tossing across to your partner on every third throw, toss **every** right hand bag across—while he does the same. Magnificent.

There are variations on this of course. You can each whistle the same tune. A different tune. He can talk. You can talk. You can memorize poems. Abbott and Costello had a two part routine called "Who's on first?" It takes about ten minutes. If you and your partner are able to recite this routine while team juggling, send me your address. I will fly there immediately.

CIRCLE JUGGLING

My own first, misguided attempts at juggling took this circular form where the objects follow one another around in one direction. Back in those days I never could get it, but a great deal of fruit and occasionally eggs went down in the effort.

Probably the most frustrating part of circle juggling is the fact that it is harder to learn than normal style juggling; but after you finally get it, it looks easier — so you don't get any credit for having gone through all that pain. The problem is that, in circle juggling, you have to keep two things in the air at once — (as per the diagram), but it looks as if there's only one. In regular juggling, the exact opposite is the case.

Anyway, so much for the editorial. The diagrams should give you a pretty good picture of how to do it. You'll start with two bags in your "best" hand — be it right or left — then toss them both up in quick succession in identical arcs heading over to your other hand. As soon as you've cleared your good hand, you'll have to cross the third bag into it in a quick, underneath throw.

Then all you have to do is keep everybody going around in a circle.

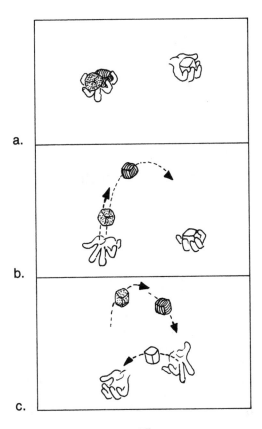

a.

b.

c.

OVERHAND GRABBING

This is just another way to make your catches. Instead of passively letting a bag land in your hand, reach up and grab it with an overhand motion. Then resume your normal juggling routine.

When you can do this consistently with either hand, you can try to toss from that overhand position (a more difficult venture). To make the toss after you have grabbed a bag, don't turn your hand back over — keep your palm down. Then flick your wrist upward, releasing the bag. This will leave your hand in a position to grab that next bag. If you can do this with every toss, you'll not only be fairly good, but you'll also have the appearance of practicing the high-speed dog paddle — which is pretty strange behavior. But by this time your friends should be used to anything.

OUTSIDE JUGGLING

This is clearly a case where a diagram is worth far more than all of my wordiness. Just look at the picture and concentrate on keeping all your tosses soft.

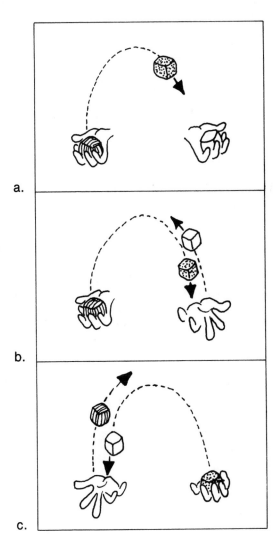

a.

b.

c.

THE "BLIND" JUGGLER

This is the most interesting trick of the lot but I include it with some reluctance because it requires one very quick handed juggler, and since quick handedness and klutziness are not often associated, this might create a problem.

Nevertheless, it's such a different kind of trick that I couldn't resist.

Stand face to face with your partner about two or three feet away. One of you is going to have to be the quick handed one while the other can be a seriously klutzy type. Settle it among yourselves as to who's who. The rest of my comments, though, will be directed to he of the quick hands.

The klutz will be the "blind" juggler, so he should close his eyes and then begin to juggle, just as if his eyes were open. But as the first bag leaves his hand, your job is to intercept it at the top of its arc and then manually (and quickly!) place it in his other hand just as he's releasing his second bag. You'll catch that one with *your* other hand and repeat the "manual exchange" in your *partner's* other hand.

The whole picture should look like this: your partner—eyes closed—will be juggling, but you'll be catching his every throw and *putting* them in his hands, right in beat with a normal juggling pattern.

The big problem is staying up with your partner and also getting your hands out of the way as his throws come up. Not easy, I admit, but still—an interesting trick.

RAZZLE DAZZLE

This is the category of pure flash. Things like making one toss from behind your back, or under your leg. Or catching your final bag by stooping over and letting it land on the back of your neck. Another one consists of popping a bag up with your knee or foot rather than doing a normal exchange.

Specific directions for all these would read like an anatomy textbook and besides, they probably wouldn't be very helpful anyway.

My only hint, if you are looking to put a little of this kind of flash in your routine, is to always heave one bag especially high before you go into whatever contortions you have in mind. You can buy yourself some needed extra time with the additional height.

TWO-IN-ONE PATTERNS

This is an entirely different way to keep three objects juggled and requires that you learn how to keep two things in the air with only one hand.

It takes some time before you can do this with any kind of consistency, so you should concentrate on learning it in the hand that you're best with. If it seems harder than normal juggling, that's because it is.

At least while you're learning, you should always keep your throws going to the inside of the bag that's dropping down. This creates a kind of circular pattern. Check the diagram carefully. Unfortunately, there aren't any secrets to learning this technique — just spread it out so you don't feel overly frustrated at any one time.

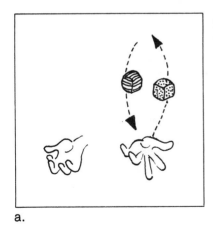 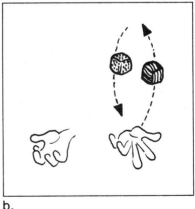

a.   b.

Notice that the bags are going in a circular kind of pattern.

51

After you feel relatively comfortable keeping two objects juggled like this, then you can bring the third bag and your other hand into the act by just tossing it up and down in time.

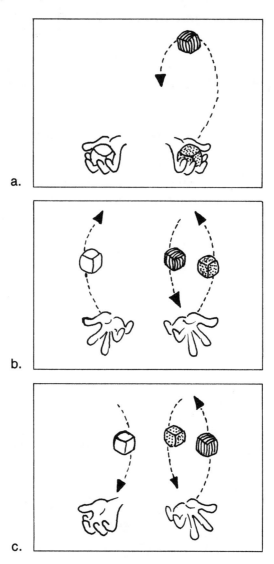

a.

b.

c.

NOTE: You can fake this pattern by keeping a hold — and never letting go — of the third bag. Then lift it and bring it down in time. Very cute.

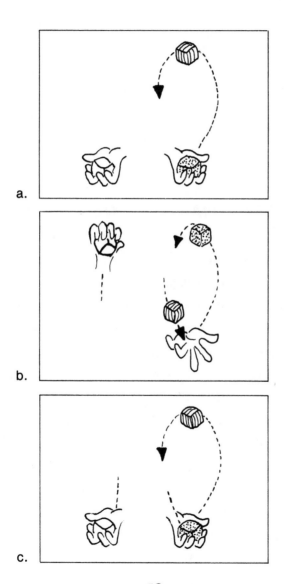

a.

b.

c.

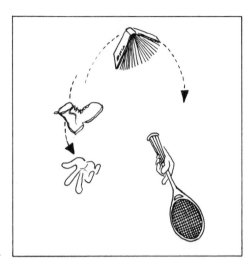

a.

JUGGLING WITH VARIOUS OBJECTS

This has always been my strongest suit, and I consider myself a near expert on the kinds of things that can be juggled.

First of all, the obvious, balls. My main hesitation about balls is that they are fine enough for juggling, but very bad for dropping. And since dropping is always a big part of my act, I have trouble with balls rolling under the furniture, dropping down storm drains, etc. Performing jugglers favor hard rubber lacrosse balls; they're expensive, but they are great for tricks where you have to bounce them off the floor rather than simply tossing them between your hands.

The diagram should give you a good idea of what's supposed to happen.

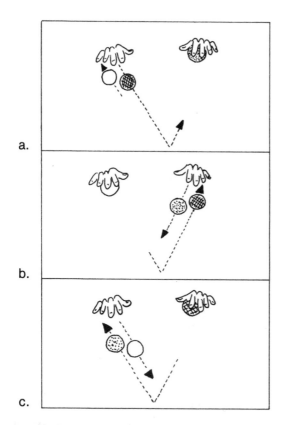

a.

b.

c.

CAUTION: If you live in a second story apartment, you probably ought to skip this one.

EDIBLES

For a beginning juggler, the produce department of any grocery store can take on a wonderful new dimension. My own favorite is the bananas. They're difficult to get the hang of at first, but even a little practice pays off quickly. If you don't try to flip them end for end, you'll find it easier.

After bananas of course there's apples, oranges, pears (when they're in season), even cantaloupes—although the weight here can be a problem.

Grapes are especially good because you can wrap up your little act by throwing them all high in the air and then catching them in your mouth. Depending on age group and interests, this can be very impressive to the person you're shopping with.

Along the same lines is the "eat-the-apple-trick" which is another great one for audience response.

Step One: Keep a careful eye out for grocery clerks.

Step Two: Take three apples and begin juggling them normally. It helps if one of them is green and the other two are red.

Step Three: When the green one gets to your right hand, make a special effort to throw it high in the air—say, about three or four feet. Keep it within reason though or you'll be visible from the next aisle.

Step Four: With the extra time you've got, bring your left-hand apple up and grab a bite out of it. If you're quick enough, you can get your hand (with bitten apple) back in place in time for the high flier to land there. You'll do an exchange and then continue juggling.

As I say, very impressive.

CAUTION: This can be a pretty messy trick, so you probably ought to dress accordingly. Also, if you don't want to eat the stem, you should twist it off at the beginning since you'll be too busy once you get started.

Just because you're out of the produce section doesn't mean there isn't anything left in the store to juggle with, but I won't list them all tediously and rob you of the pleasure of discovery.

EXCEPTION: Eggs. This is a controversial subject because drops are especially hard to recover from gracefully; but, at the same time, you don't have the roll-away problem. Use your own judgement here.

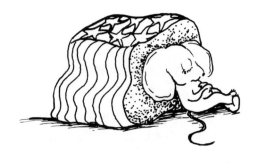

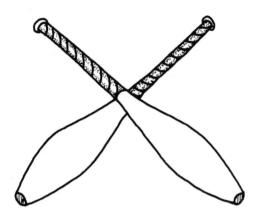

JUGGLING CLUBS

Juggling clubs are those things that look like bowling pins. For most people who've managed to achieve a state of bean bag competency, clubs are the next place to go. At the jugglers' conventions these days, clubs outnumber balls or bean bags 10 to 1. The reason for their popularity is simple: team juggling is more fun than solo juggling, and club passing is the best kind of team juggling.

Performing jugglers have always tended to favor clubs because all that flying lumber looks so impressive. Not to mention visible from the back of the hall.

Fortunately for the rest of us, they're not nearly as tricky as they seem. In fact, once you're past the original "what-in-the-world-do-I-do-with-these-things" hump, you'll find they're actually harder to drop than bean bags.

You can either make juggling clubs at home, or buy them directly through the mail. The ordering information is in the back of the book.

The ingredients for home-made juggling pins are: three, old, plastic, one quart bleach bottles and three cut-off pieces of a wooden broomstick. The diagram should show you how to put them all together.

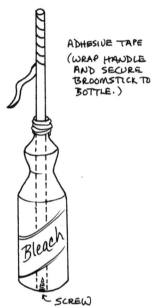

ADHESIVE TAPE (WRAP HANDLE AND SECURE BROOMSTICK TO BOTTLE.)

Bleach

← SCREW

STEP I: The Flip

This is it. The basic move in club juggling. You have to burn it into your alpha-wave subconscious neuro-patterns.

Start with one club held as per the diagram. Flip it over to your other hand—it should peak just a little over your head—and catch it around the neck. Don't clonk yourself. You know you've done it right when you don't have to move your catching hand. The club just lands in it.

3.

2.

1.

Ten minutes later.

Boring, isn't it? Pick up the second club and add some challenge.

Doing an exchange with two clubs requires two good, relaxed, accurate, flips. Just as the first flip peaks out and starts down, toss the other one just to the inside of the dropping club. (Identical pattern to bean bag juggling.)

You'll probably go through some of the same panic responses that you first went through with bean bags. The desperate catches, the weird throws . . . familiar ground by now. The only new variable in the flip is the speed at which you turn the club. When you've turned it too quickly or too slowly, catching it around the neck becomes a true challenge.

Practice, practice, practice . . .

Step 1

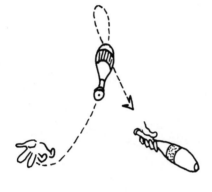 Step 2

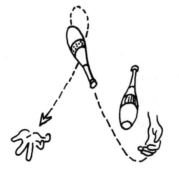 Step 3

 Step 4

Once you can manage two clubs, of course, three becomes an irresistible goal. Getting started with three seems a bit awkward at first because putting two clubs in one hand seems such a squeeze. Check the diagram for the right grip.

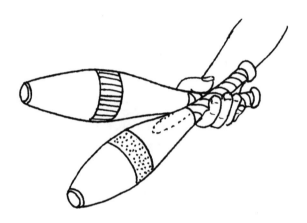

Just like you did with three bean bags, start with the hand that has two things in it. Count out loud as you toss each club and when (and if) you get to three, stop. That's a jug. You're on your way to the circus.

Step 1

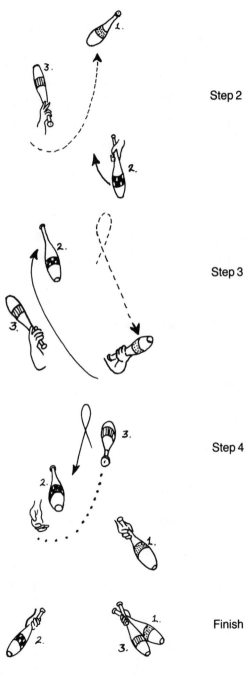

Step 2

Step 3

Step 4

Finish

65

CLUB PASSING

Although you may have your doubts at first, there will come a time when you can juggle with three clubs with reasonable ease. At that point, you should start looking for a partner, because team juggling is the name of the game. Passing clubs with a partner, (or partners) is a lot of fun. There's no way around it.

The steps to learning the basic club pass are identical to those outlined for bean bag passing (page 36). You'll just need a little more clear space to work in. Start with three clubs and two people. Spread yourselves out about 12 feet and warm yourselves up with the following exercise:

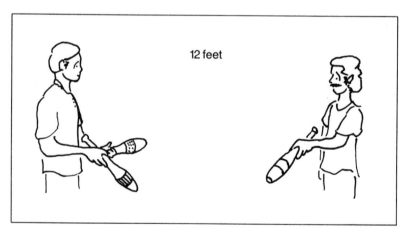

Person A
Holding two

Person B
At the ready, with one

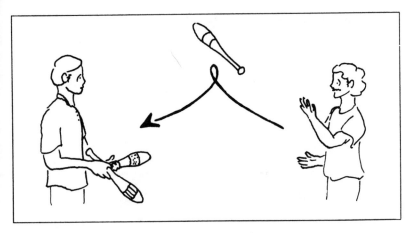

Person A
Begins juggling with
the club that . . .

Person B
. . . tosses (from his
right, to partners left)

The second exercise requires two people and four clubs:

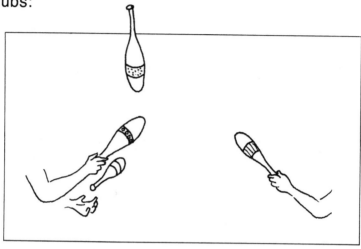

Person A
Juggling merrily away

Person B
Poised

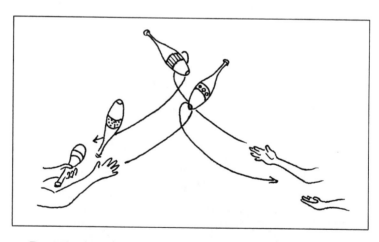

Person A
Tosses across (from his
right hand) while . . .

Person B
. . . tosses from his right

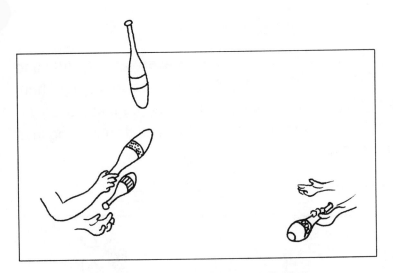

Person A
Back to normal juggling

Person B
Left holding the club

Once you can manage this second exercise fairly well, you're on the brink of success. Pick up the remaining club. Now both of you should be standing there, each nervously clutching three clubs. Start juggling in sync. The best way to do this (all the pros do it this way) is to lift your clubs chest high your partner does the same, then on a signal, both of you bring them down and start juggling.

Count every time a club leaves your _right_ hand: 1 . . . 2 . . . 3. On three, flip to your partner's right hand while he does the same. Continue juggling, counting, and tossing on every third right-hand throw. Bring in an audience.

Step 1.   Juggle in sync. Count on every right-hand toss.

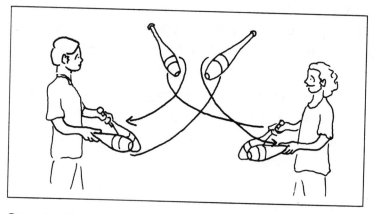

Step 2.   Everybody tosses from their right hands on 3 count.

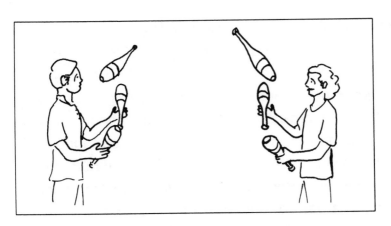

*Step 3. (Ideal) Everyone catches the passes and
goes back to juggling*

*Step 4. (Reality) No one catches anything. One
club hits shoulder. Another bounces
off shin.*

HIGHER MATH IN CLUB PASSING

Let's say you've defied everyone's predictions and actually learned how to do this trick. Now you are into the world of serious craziness. Jugglers hold conventions where crowds of them pass clubs back and forth like a choreographed pie fight. If you can juggle between two people, adding any additional number just changes the direction you're tossing to and catching from. The pattern and individual moves are identical. All you'll need is split vision.

As long as you're into these advanced realms, you can experiment with the timing of your pattern. Don't limit yourselves to every third throw. Flip every other right-hand throw, or every right-hand throw . . . or you can try the ultimate,

Random Passing

Two of you juggle along, then, whenever the urge strikes, toss across without the slightest warning. Your partner now has about one panic-stricken second to do the same before he has to catch yours and continue juggling. Extremely tricky.

There's no limit to where you can take club passing. For most jugglers, this is where they spend the rest of their juggling lives. It combines the camaraderie of team sports with the solo skills of juggling. From here it goes on forever. You can contact the International Jugglers Association (Box 29, Kenmore, NY 14217) if you'd like to attend a convention and get into one of the pie fights. Don't worry, no matter how lame you are, jugglers of every skill level attend.

Tricks with Clubs

Let your imagination roam. Anything you can do with bean bags, you can do with clubs. Behind the back. Between the legs. All that stuff.

You can toss them without the flip ("floaters") for a little extra challenge. Or you can double or triple flip them ("spinners").

One trick unique to clubs is the "kick-up." _Very_ impressive—but it'll be at least a couple of days before you'll even begin to get the hang of it. The idea is to pick up a dropped club with your foot and flip it back up into a juggling pattern. (No more humiliation as you bend over to pick up drops.)

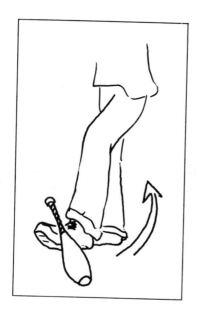 

The Kick-up

For the Kick-up, you have to rest the neck of the club over the top of your foot. Lifting the club from this position may seem impossible, but the trick is to catch the knob on your shin as you swing your foot out and up (not unlike the dog-sees-hydrant move.) Properly done, the club will come up with a single flip.

Juggling Various Strange Club-like Objects

After you've mastered the basic club flip, a whole new category of weird things becomes jugglable. Flying hatchets, torches, small chainsaws, flaming knives . . . that sort of thing.

Personally, I tend to shy away from sharp things that are on fire. I do have a specialty though—rubber chickens. And plumbers' helpers (those big rubber suction things). I have a "rubber chicken-plumbers' helper-and-egg routine" that is just about ready for prime time.

NUMBERS JUGGLING

This is the section where I'm finally going to talk about juggling with more than 3 objects. I've deliberately saved it for the end because it's a special case, with mental health implications.

At this point, you are probably juggling three objects (clubs, bean bags, chinaware, rubber chickens . . .) with casual flair. You feel a certain sense of pride and accomplishment. Your friends, though, are bored. They want 4.

Learning how to juggle with 4 is not all that tricky. I'll go over the steps here in a minute, but before you start in on it, you should recognize that 4 is not what your friends _really_ want. What they really want is one more than whatever you can do. This is the numbers game trap.

Learning how to juggle with 3 objects, on a scale of 1 to 10, is a two. Learning how to juggle with 4 objects, is a 5. Learning how to juggle with 5, figure 34. Beyond that I can't count that high. Enrico Rastelli, an Italian juggler who was active 50 years ago, is considered history's finest juggler. He reportedly could juggle 11 objects. He also practiced 12 hours a day.

There are a zillion tricks and variations with three objects and passing patterns. More than enough to occupy a lifetime.

Having said all that, I know that there are those of you out there who must know how it is done. It is for their doomed sakes that I set these instructions down.

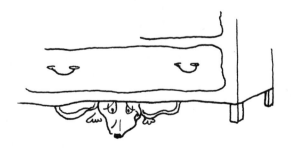

Four Object Juggling

In order to juggle with four, you will have to develop your "off" hand in the same way that you developed your "good" hand for the "two-in-one" patterns. If you're right-handed, that means you'll be working with your left—and vice versa.

Clearly, this is going to take some time. Your object is to keep two bean bags juggled with only one hand (your "off" hand) and do it under control.

If you can get over that hurdle, then you'll have reached the point of no return, so I might as well play the rest of this out.

A. Put two bags in each hand. Practice for a moment keeping the two in your right hand going.

B. Then stop and practice with your left.

C. Then (deep breath) practice with both hands simultaneously. You do **not** cross any bags between hands.

NOTE: Don't start with both hands simultaneously. Stagger your starts one...two. This is a bit hard to describe, but the idea is that your hands will be going up and down and making exchanges alternately rather than simultaneously.

A.

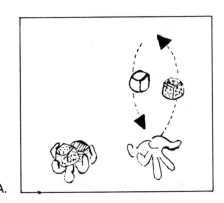

B.

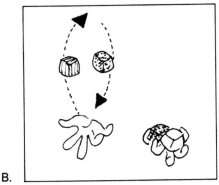

C.

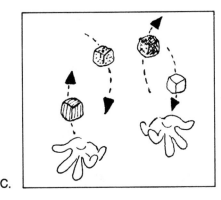

79

Five Object Juggling

The black belt of juggling. I have never heard of anyone learning how to juggle five objects in less than 3 months effort. Consider yourself warned.

Put three bags in one hand, two in the other, and stand over a big bed. Starting with your three bag hand, toss one up in a high, perfectly accurate arc over to your other hand. But before it even peaks out, toss one out of your other hand in another perfectly accurate arc. And then (are you still there?) toss the second bag out of your first hand.

So, if we freeze the action for a second here, this is what it looks like. There are three things in the air— all perfectly thrown on arcs that pass one another, but are nevertheless **identical** in terms of height and width.

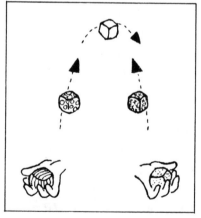

Their arrangement over your hands should be as illustrated. Two bags are still being held.

Now, as each flying bag drops into your hand, you'll

exchange it with the flier—and in this way (theoretically) you should be able to keep everything going.

The pattern used in juggling five things is identical to the pattern used in juggling three, but I can't emphasize enough the difference between having three things in the air and having one.

The difficulty, as will soon become apparent, is that each and every toss has to peak out at *exactly* the same height. Otherwise, the pattern will disintegrate. For a good long time, this will not seem even remotely possible.

There are a couple of things that might help in training. At first, don't make any effort at catching. Throw all five bean bags up, in as good a pattern as you can, and then watch and listen as they hit the bed. The three that left your right hand should fall into a tight cluster directly underneath your left hand, and the two that left your left hand should do the same under your right hand. (They won't, of course, but they should.) You should also be able to hear five distinct "plops" indicating that all five bags kept their original spacing.

An alternative to a big bed is a partner engaged in the same 5-object quest. The two of you should stand face to face, a foot or so apart. Let's say you're the one holding the bags. Throw them all up in your best pattern and then forget about them. Your partner should try to catch them all. If your tosses were reasonably accurate, this is not impossible. Then reverse the process. Back and forth. (Credit to Dave Finnigan and Roger Dollarhide, dedicated jugglers both, for this idea.)

This would be an excellent trick to work on if you ever get a job on a desert island or in a lighthouse.

MAIL ORDER INFORMATION

Juggling for the Complete Klutz $9.⁹⁵

The most popular book on juggling ever published. A 65 page volume, written for the mashed-finger and dented-shin crowd. By John Cassidy & B.C. Rimbeaux. Illustrated by Diane Waller. Comes with with three juggling bags.

Juggling Bags $2.⁰⁰ ea. $5.⁰⁰ per set of 3

Colorful, hand-sewn bean bags of calico and denim . . . ideal size and weight for juggling. They don't bounce around, they won't roll away, and they won't make a mess on the floor. No klutz is complete without them.

Ultimate Juggling Bags $8.⁰⁰ per set of 3

Sewn with crushed red velour (instead of calico and denim). Appropriate for most formal occasions.

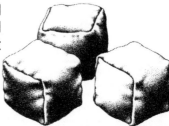

Juggling Clubs $21.⁵⁰ per set of 3

Three injection molded polyethylene juggling clubs. Basically the same shape as bowling pins except they're balanced and designed for juggling. Red, blue, and yellow colors.

Professional Style Clubs $49.⁵⁰ per set of 3

For the semi-serious juggler. Polyethylene construction, with a padded knob, bottom, extra handle and a two-tone gold and white finish. Barnum and Bailey material.

Juggling Balls $8.⁵⁰ per set of 3

Three lacrosse-style, hard rubber balls with a ribbed, easy-to-grip surface. Each set contains one red, one blue and one yellow ball.

Juggling Rings $15.⁰⁰ per set of 3

Manufactured for us, these are die-cut and smooth-machined out of polyethylene plastic. Indestructible, light and colorful, they are 13" in outside diameter. Sergei Ignatov, the Michael Jordan of juggling, always uses rings when keeping more than 11 objects going at once.

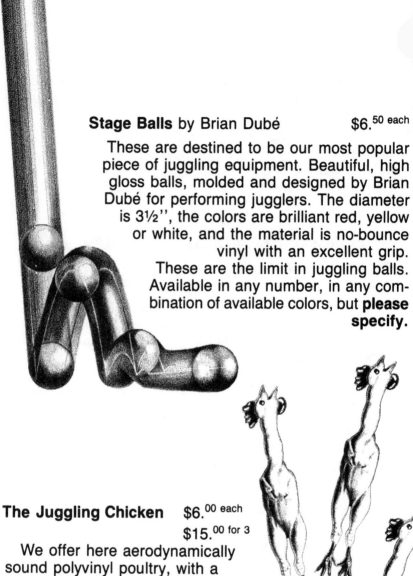

Stage Balls by Brian Dubé — $6.⁵⁰ each

These are destined to be our most popular piece of juggling equipment. Beautiful, high gloss balls, molded and designed by Brian Dubé for performing jugglers. The diameter is 3½'', the colors are brilliant red, yellow or white, and the material is no-bounce vinyl with an excellent grip. These are the limit in juggling balls. Available in any number, in any combination of available colors, but **please specify.**

The Juggling Chicken — $6.⁰⁰ each — $15.⁰⁰ for 3

We offer here aerodynamically sound polyvinyl poultry, with a style and flair that speak for themselves. You may use them for juggling, as decorations around your home or patio, or just for general household purposes.

MAIL ORDER BLANK

Quantity	Description	Price
	Add $1.00 for Postage	
	Total Enclosed (check or money order)	

Name _____

Street _____

Address _____

J Klutz Enterprises / 2170 Staunton Ct. / Palo Alto CA 94306

FREE CATALOGUE FORM

The *FLYING APPARATUS CATALOGUE* is filled with unicycles, juggling paraphernalia, kites, boomerangs and who knows what all. It's available free for the asking.

Name _____

Street _____

Town/State _____

Zip _____

J

Please include check or money order and mail to:
Klutz Enterprises / 2170 Staunton Ct. / Palo Alto CA 94306

MAIL ORDER BLANK

Quantity	Description	Price
	Add $1.00 for Postage	
	Total Enclosed (check or money order)	

Name _____

Street _____

Address _____

J   Klutz Enterprises / 2170 Staunton Ct. / Palo Alto CA 94306

FREE CATALOGUE FORM

The *FLYING APPARATUS CATALOGUE* is filled with unicycles, juggling paraphernalia, kites, boomerangs and who knows what all. It's available free for the asking.

Name _____

Street _____

Town/State _____

Zip _____

J

Please include check or money order and mail to:
Klutz Enterprises / 2170 Staunton Ct. / Palo Alto CA 94306